A Part was Given and an Angel was Born

By Rozanne Nathalie

Illustrations/Graphics
by Jennifer Lofchie and Bruce Sulzberg

Beaver's Pond Press, Inc.
Edina, Minnesota

A PART WAS GIVEN AND AN ANGEL WAS BORN © copyright 2002 by Rozanne Nathalie. All rights reserved. No part of this book may be reproduced in any form whatsoever, by photography or xerography or by any other means, by broadcast or transmission, by translation into any kind of language, nor by recording electronically or otherwise, without permission in writing from the author, except by a reviewer, who may quote brief passages in critical articles or reviews.

ISBN 1-931646-78-3

Printed in the United States of America

First Printing: September 2002

06 05 04 03 02   6 5 4 3 2 1

Beaver's Pond Press, Inc.

5125 Danen's Drive
Edina, MN 55439-1465
(952) 829-8818
www.beaverspondpress.com

to order, visit *midwestbookhouse.com* or call 1-877-430-0044. Quantity discounts available.

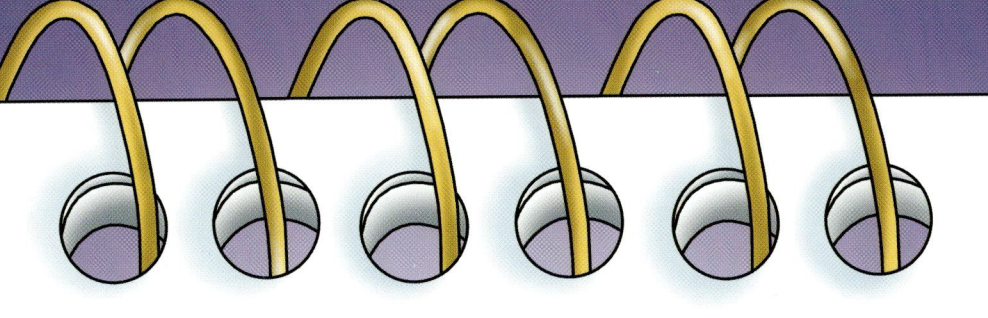

Note from Author

Dear Parents,

I have written these books for you to use as a tool. They are to assist you in explaining to your children the miracle of how they came into your lives. This series was born from 10 years of extraordinary experiences with incredible people such as you. They are truly my labors of love.

I recognize that there are many different, remarkable and beautiful family units that exist; however, for the sake of simplicity these books are written using the traditional "Mommy and Daddy." However, they can easily be adapted to be read with one or the other, by changing "we" to "I," "our" to "my," etc.

This is a keepsake book that your child will treasure as they get older. It will forever remind them of all the love that it took to help them come into this world. Please use the last page of this book to write a letter to your child so that your words of love will be indelibly imprinted in your child's life.

My sincere congratulations,

Rozanne Nathalie

So much love went into making you.
The kind of love that is so true.

You are so special. Do you know why?
We had a great team, your Daddy and I.

We tried and we tried, but you did not come.
We dreamed of you, you were our special one.

Our hearts were heavy and our souls incomplete.
We had to have you no matter how hard the feat.

So one day we went to the doctor to see,
What was the trouble?
Is there something wrong with me?

DOCTOR'S OFFICE

Come on in . . .
or
Look us up!

FREE LOLLIPOPS!

The Doctor was nice and he could see we were sad.
He told us "Cheer up, things aren't that bad."

We'd be able to have you, he knew that we would.
But there was a part in Mommy that just didn't
work as it should.

What we needed to do was find another part.
That was our problem, then we could start.

We were so thrilled to find out there were ways.
This was the best news we had heard in days.

But how would we find this part that we need?
Was there someone so special that would help
us succeed?

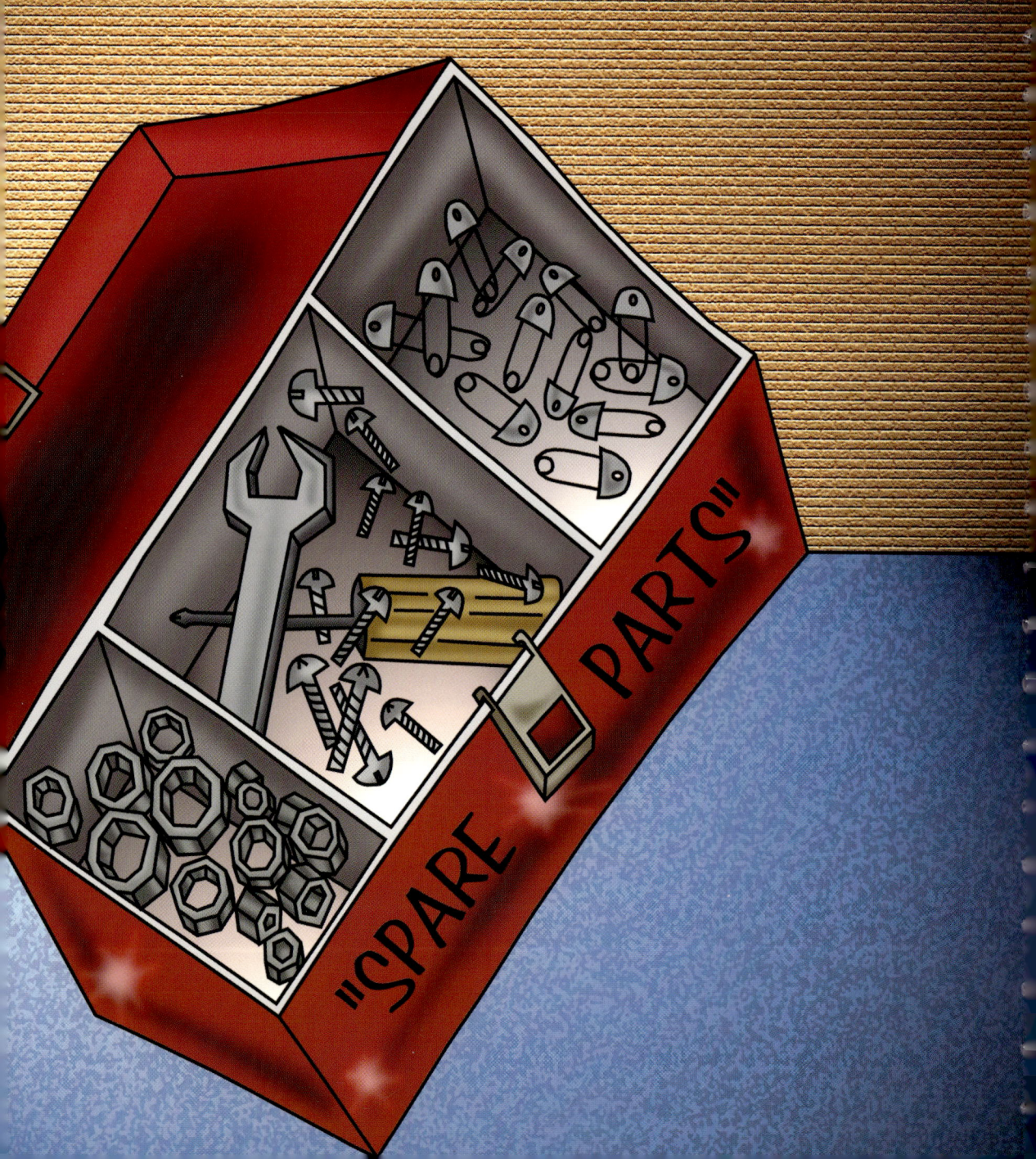

"SPARE PARTS"

We looked and looked . . . but we couldn't find anyone
   with that part.
Until one day, a very special lady with a heart,
Said "I'll help you, I'll help you, let me give this to you.
I'll share my part so that your dream can come true."

We couldn't believe that it was actually to be,
With everyone's help, we'd have you, Daddy and me.

We all worked together as an incredible team.
And before we knew it, we had made you, our dream!

You were in my tummy, and I could feel you there.
I would talk to you always about the love and the care...

That everyone felt, and this was true.
You're our special little angel, and we love you.

to baby . . .

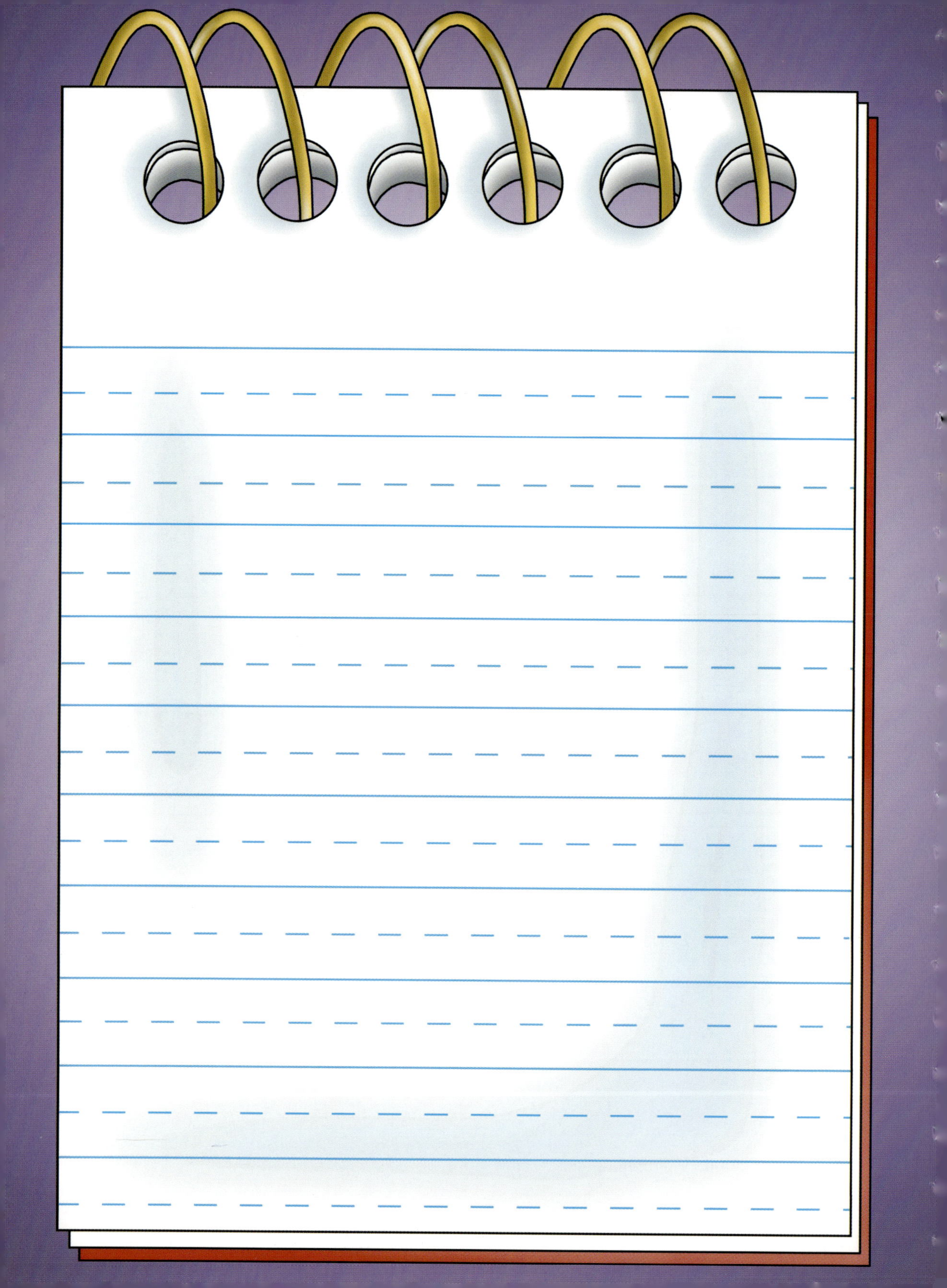

As many of your experiences reflect, it takes a collaborative effort of a dedicated team to help make dreams come true... and this project is no different. What started as a dream is now a reality thanks to the generous support of Serono Inc., makers of infertility pharmaceuticals. They saw the vision, recognized the need, and worked diligently with me to help bring these books to you. I know that I speak for more than just myself when I say "Thank you Serono."

serono
biotech & beyond

Tell Your Child

Special Stories for Special Children
www.TellYourChild.com